Thanks to the universe
For letting me be
I dedicate this book
To my entity
And of course to my
British family

TEMPLE FIELDS

PUBLISHED

BY BRITISHPOEMS.CO.UK

PRINTED

BY TYSON PRINTING.CO.UK

ISBN NUMBER

978-0-9574690-0-6

COVER DESIGN

KISSAGENCY.BIZ

CONTENTS

BRILLIANT BRITAIN

We make all the best music it's got global appeal
We're mostly straight talking and we tend to keep it real
We're honest reliable dependable and punctual
Quiet easygoing understanding intellectual
We're great at making sausages and cheese and bread and pies
Naive and daft and honest we're not great at telling lies
Amiable hospitable sociable and brainy
Go about our business even when it's rainy
Indiscriminate diplomatic charitable good losers
Lovely cakes with dairy cream Mr Bean and great boozers

The comedy's top notch it's up there with the best
Our creativity's pretty good if not better than the rest
Tolerant and patient organized and shy
Conservative and underplayed our humour's mainly dry
We're great at making spotted dick and chips and peas and gravy
You know our brilliant soldiers are just brilliant like our navy
Generous and lovable genuine and kind
Helpful undemanding and popular you'll find

Accommodating considerate gregarious and good-natured
We've fantastic tasty pasties pretty flowers and no hatred

Our countryside's amazing there's cows and pigs and sheep
And all of them are grazing on land that's ours to keep
Back streets and side streets towpaths and cobbles
Cute villages and historic castles and exceptional novels
We're great at making sherry trifle soups and stews and butter
We'd never have our fellow man left lying in the gutter
Affable laughable sensitive and gentle
Hospitable realistic if at times a little mental
Eccentric traditional a stunning range of trees
Fantastic radio in our hospitals bumble bees and different teas

We love our national football we're not that great any more
Now it's medals at triathlons and heptathlons galore
Bradley Sebastian Motty and Murray
With great people like this we've no need to worry
We're thoughtful with our pets and we clean up their mess
The Royal family's our asset we don't judge how you dress

Sensible efficient organised and calm
Diligent intelligent and rarely without charm
Artistic educated culturally diverse
Some of the best universities in the whole universe

We're orderly fashionable respectable full of flu
If there's anything we're great at we sure know how to queue
Bashful friendly courteous on the roads
We've otters moles slugs and snails and a variety of toads
Manicured lay-bys and the famous NHS
Miss Marple and the Beeb maybe you couldn't care less?
But we invented nearly everything from golfing to the web
So as far as celebrity countries go we must be the top celeb'
You know I hate the weather here but even so I'm smitten
The quality of a life for me is a life made in Brilliant Great Britain

YOUNG MUMS

Hated slated just for being young
The curse of the young mum
No wonder she's highly strung

We label her we blame her
For the state of our affairs
Why is age on the front page?
C'mon let's not split the hairs

I know girls who've given birth
Even in their teens
Doesn't mean they're not great mums
Just means they're full of beans

Show me a mother tell me her age
What am I supposed to think?
I'm confused by the importance of years these days
What? She can't even have a drink?

Maybe she *is* single and maybe she's not
It's up to you to stop yourself
From trying to join that dot
Give them a chance to express themselves
Surely expectations can bend
You might even find she's a really nice girl
And she could even be your friend

Coz young mums are given some really bad press
It's the papers the TV the journos I guess
Well I'm not subscribing to this alleged mess
For me it's a worrying trend

We're driving young mums round the bend

I'd tick the box that says **END.**

OUTSIDE OF LONDON

Interesting characters kids in the streets
Hospitable shopkeepers tastier meats
Quality textiles genuine fashion
Original artwork more passion
Finer football with better songs
Quieter churches bigger throngs
Darker cemeteries statelier homes
Larger collections of garden gnomes
Cleaner air greener fields
Purer water superior deals
More relaxed less stress
Less rubble less mess
Brighter faces shinier smiles
Traffic jams for shorter miles
Not as noisy minor pollution
Buses with seats less intrusion
Wilder animals for example the skunk
Realer ales that get you proper drunk

Palatable pies fresher fish
Authentic food authentic dish
Stewier stews funner fairs
Funnier comics n blanker stares
More rain minus pain
Smaller overdraft less of a drain
Fewer homeless out and about
Woolier sheep increased doubt
Less scabies thicker gravies
Crisper chips uglier babies
Topper tunes more bangin' beats
Chirpier birds n sweeter tweets
Less superficial a little bit deeper
Friendlier folk and it's a damn sight cheaper
A lot more difficult to get barred
Won't ever need an Oyster card
You're not gonna find the going hard

Coz you're Outside of London

DOG NATION

We're a nation of dog lovers
We've got pooches with godmothers
Extreme with our affection against vivisection
We treat 'em like they're our brothers

We let them in our cars
In our homes in our heads
We allow them on our sofas
And even in our beds

The British mutt has all it needs
They're treated just like royalty
The luckiest dogs in all the land
They're experts when it comes to loyalty

Our dogs and us we never argue
He never answers back
We clean up his pooh in the middle of the street
Occasionally wiping his crack

Not once has he ever questioned us
Or told us we're all fools
I'm fond of his paws his nose his tail
Even the smell of his stools

A world without the British hound
Would be boring and lifeless and blue
Then again the company of humans these days
I'd rather talk to the dog than with you

Because doggy I'm in love with you

What would we EVER do?

B B B BALTIC IN THE BATHROOM

I’m content when I’m closing curtains
I’m joyous closing doors
I get a kick out of triple glazing
And heating under floors

Rads n dials n thermos
Basically just turn me on
Give me flow and return baby
And I get what’s goin' on

I love the thought of wind and rain
And storms with tons of force
I know life wouldn’t be worth living
Without a damp proof course

I adore just scraping windscreens
And freezin’ toilet seats
I’m smiling wearing layers
Along with chilly sheets

It makes me go all tingly
When I ponder winter nights
The dewdrops on your nose my love
And all that lovely ice

The notion of diggin' out
Makes my heart skip two beats
The pain of lovely sunshine
The pleasure of darkened weeks

I'm ecstatic about hot water bottles
And boarding out the loft
Yes I'm fond of immersion heaters
You must think I'm goin' soft

I'm excited by insulation
Yet angry about draughts
I've tried to get some counselling
But all I get are laughs

Friends don't understand me
My gran's the only one
The two of us perversely
Sitting well out of the sun

She's ninety-six this Christmas
And if you want to go to 'eaven
She reckons you need some decent slippers
And definitely Economy Seven

She says we were born to suffer lad
I'm inclined to share her view
I'm sure we *were* meant to suffer
I mean *love* the British weather
Don't you?

THE GREAT BRITISH FAIR

Fat slags n drunken lads
Dodgy burgers n cheap fags
Faded tats n pierced nips
Smelly hotdogs n greasy chips

Chained up dogs n caravans
Shaven 'eads n fake tans
Fair's in town it's time for fun!
Fiver a ride?
Think you've been done

Pissin' it down looking for shelter
Burn yer arse on the 'Elter Skelter
Rickety rides and haunted houses
Ketchup n mustard down their blouses

The louder you scream the faster you go
The more you drink the more you throw!

But fair's in town so it's time for fun!
The rings don't fit you know you've been done

Cuddly toys you've no chance of winnin'
Get 'em home they're ready for binnin'
Archaic arcades and penny slots
Flashin' lights n prams n tots

Penniless parents screaming kids
Heads down looking for quids
Fair's in town it's bound to be fun!
Everyone's out even yer mum!

Piss poor dodgems n soap dodgers
Scrawny blokes n old codgers
Toffee apples popcorn n beer
I'm on the waltzers feelin' queer

Pools of puke n tottering birds
Rock 'ard dart boards n fresh dog turds

The fair's in town ya comin' out?
Doubt it pal I'll give you a shout

When I was little the fair was great
Now it just feels like somethin' I 'ate

Candy Floss and Hook a Duck?

The great British fair?

Who gives a f...?

ANYONE SPEAK ENGLISH?

Don't need to learn another language do I?
The world speaks English wherever I fly
And no matter how hard I try
Other languages just seem to pass me by
I'm English me speak English you see
Can't communicate verbally
Unless it's English then I'm dumbfounded
My head's full of mush it feels overcrowded

Gobbledigook makes no sense to me
Please speak the Queen's English ideally RP
I'm not ignorant me honestly
In England the English don't educate you see
Think I'm substandard genetically
Learning new lingos failing pathetically

So unless it's English then I'll be dumbfounded
Other languages for me in mystery they're shrouded

Scottish and Welsh can be hard enough
Never mind the grammar punctuation and stuff
It's great is our English it's a piece of cake
No tenses third persons won't make yer brain ache
As long you're talking in my native tongue
I can't really see what else can go wrong

So it's got to be English or else I'm dumbfounded
Speak foreign to me my head it gets clouded

When I go on holiday the first thing I ask
Is do you speak English? Yep that's the first task
Find me a friend who understands what I'm saying
Or I get frustrated my nerves will start fraying
And the missus and kids will sit their red-faced
Clueless and gormless dictionaries just in case

So please please speak English or else we're dumbfounded
If ya can't speak our English
Then you should be grounded

MARKET TOWN STARE

Boarded up shut up shop the white washed windows
This town's a flop
Empty pubs the streets are bare
There's no more work the men just stare...
Into space

On the market place there's three stalls left
Used to be hundreds but now bereft
It's the retail park on the edge of town
That Starbucks Primark and stupid Clown
There's no more work the job centre's full
Men are just staring it's mindless and dull

Can't get it fixed so replace it with new
I knew Mr Fixit but now he's with you
At home on the couch nothing to do
Despair at not having to repair
So he continues to stare at the box

Customer care and the neighbourhood watches
Delivery boys pushing pizzas through boxes
Pedestrianised sanitised regeneration
Nothing but red tape and daft regulation
Hoodies and homeless boarders and mopeds
Parks full of piedos and addicts and dope heads
Can't walk the streets for fear of abuse
Paranoid anger idiots let loose
Indoors on Xbox Facebook and Twitter
Littering lives with a zombiefied jitter
And the kids just stare into space...
And the families just slot into place

Councils so anal they drive you insane
Recycling our minds it's important to save
Our planet with millions of bins cost the earth
What on earth is this town? There's nothing of worth
What happened to the post office the pool and the school?
It's all turned to concrete and parking you fools
So just stare at your screens and drool
And stare into space you fool

Twitching of curtains checking our streets
No more bobbies just repetitive beats
The Wacky Warehouse has taken our tots
Buy only at Argos and only job lots
Pound shops and cafes the world's drinking tea
We stare at each other
Are you staring at me?

Off to the city now that's where I work
Our local buses and trains they don't work
The traffic piles up and I just look up
And continue to stare into space...

When I was a kid there was stuff to do
But now it seems like we haven't a clue
Communities split divided and hit
Like an unsurprising bolt from the blue

What happened to this place?
No Woolworths no Comet
The thought of it all makes me want to vomit

In spite of it all what's happened to us all?

The community to me and to you?

And we all just stare into space...

And our lives just slot into place

THE GREAT BRITISH BREAKFAST

It's half past seven I'm in heaven
The smell of bacon I'm about to dine
The kettle's just boiled it's totally time
For the Great British breakfast

Porridge oats with a dash of honey
A gallon of juice you ready Mr Tummy?
The Great British breakfast on its way
Nice n heavy sets you up for the day

Cereals Corn Flakes Rice Crispies sugar
Tinned fruit and yoghurt for the chubby little bugger
Rounds of toast n butter jams and conserves
Nothing less than the average builder deserves
Oatcakes Eccles cakes cup cakes and pies
White sliced or granary baps and barms before your eyes

Poached eggs boiled eggs and soldiers we're fed
Not forgetting scrambled and why not eggy bread?

Frying pan fried tomato fried bread of course
Full cream milk from dairy cows loads of ketchup n brown sauce

Cumberland sausages pork sausages bangers and baked beans
I 'aven't missed a British breakfast since me early teens
This heart attack on a plate please don't make me die
Though I could think of worse ways to meet my maker in the sky

Smoked bacon back bacon rindless and rashers
Hash browns mushrooms salt n pepper dashes
Black puddin' white puddin' now it's getting serious
This fullest of English breakfasts is making me delirious

Mornings without you it's like a turkey without stuffin'
Before I quit I might as well 'ave one last chocolate muffin

I've finished the lot can't move off the spot
Swilled it all down with tea more happy than can be
You're part of our family

You're the Great British breakfast

RETROGRADE

I remember streets without speed humps police without guns and
a time when it was posh to eat pasta
I remember when you could only *squeeze* a tube of toothpaste
I remember when Snaps were two pence I remember Rowntree's Counters
Atari and I remember Crown Court in black and white
I remember when I couldn't call people unless they were at home
And they couldn't call me
I remember when the word 'text' meant some writing in a book
I remember no seat belts in cars and sharing the bath water with my brother
I was always first because I was always first to bed
The bottom bunk I seem to remember

I remember Tiswas and thinking Morning Worship was definitely on and
why weren't there battleships instead of old people singing?
I remember Moon boots like they were yesterday
I remember Ugg boots and wondering what all the fuss was about
I remember n-gauge trains swing ball as the new craze and JPS cigarettes
When they first came out
I remember when you could smoke inside drink on the streets and get two

ounces of hundreds and thousands
I remember a world without fast food – except for fish and chips
I remember the Elvis newsflash Lester Piggott being done for tax Bobby Sands' funeral and George Best drinking a mountain of champagne
I remember pinhole cameras iron filings experiments and Starsky's trainers

Can you remember the feeling you got listening to that cereal go snap crackle and pop for the first time?
Do you remember what it felt like to run across the street without looking?
And alone?

I bet you can't remember the experience I had going to watch Kenny Hibbert at the Molyneux

Some memories are all yours no-one else's
Not even if you wanted it so

I bet you'd all forgotten about the halfpence piece already
And I'd be happy to wager that years go by without you remembering
Brains faggots or Kick Start on BBC2 or Hilda's three ducks

It's what I realise I *don't* remember that I can get into

For instance do you remember when you last couldn't see a camera?
Do you remember a day when a camera couldn't see you?
I remember when a gollywog on a jam jar was just a cute character on a jam jar
I remember thinking I'd miss him when he went
I remember my gran saying that silly egg on her mantelpiece would be worth a lot of money one day
And I remember not believing her

I remember not believing her because it was the only time I can remember that I didn't believe her

I remember when a million pound house was unheard of
Even for a footballer
Trevor Francis maybe but who will be the first billion pound footballer - to be remembered?

I'd like to say it couldn't happen in my lifetime but...I remember there's no point in saying that

It's true certain minutia in our lives are destined *not* to be in the re-memory banks of future generations

They will never know how it felt for example to wear tight-fitting football shorts and they will never understand the taste of warm school milk or even the feel of greaseproof toilet paper

Some of the above *are* memories
Some of them are lost memories

All but forgotten for me akin to memories from the Great War
Some things are *not* memories at all
They live on leaving the useless tasteless and time consuming behind in the unfashionable gutter
They do live on
For instance the BBC Ready Brek and the Archers
The speaking clock and trains being late
If I say the transcendental phrases like The Curly Wurly or Murray Walker I think you know where we stand

Some things *will* live forever and so never actually be remembered

I take pleasure in remembering

Especially over those younger than me because technically I've more memories than them
That makes me more qualified in the memory department
I take pleasure in knowing a feeling or sensation of something that people in the future will never have the satisfaction of remembering

Great things can and do die and once a generation passes so does 'stuff'
For instance Blankety Blank with Les Dawson
Monty Python and Not The Nine O'Clock News

I can't wait to tell my grandchildren about the Evel Knievel motorbike and see their shiny little faces light up with wonder

Just like I remember mine doing

And when they're older about the collapse of communism in Russia and the fall of the wall and a time when everything *wasn't* made in China

And try to explain to them the warm sense of being just clutching a hot water bottle in the dead of winter

Imagine trying to explain to future generations what life was like before remote controls for TV's before Eastenders before Easyjet and The Champions League and combi boilers?

I can remember that world

Yes I remember when *all* telephone boxes were red and seriously people used them

Think about it
They're all around us
Things feelings experiences
All to remember
Just try and remember
And it feels good even warm sometimes
And if you can't remember then maybe it's not even worth remembering

With my memories I'm happy content fullfilled

With my memories I am never alone

Remember to spare a thought for people who have no memory at all and consequently have nothing to remember and remember nothing

Imagine remembering nothing

BOOZE YOU LOSE

I like a pint
I'll drink an ale even if it's stale or pale
Always hear me shout for another stout
Bitter and twisted call me what you want
Lager than life cider not so rosé
Haven't seen the wife
For ages

Never fear the beer's here
Wine's fine for a tipple
Feelin' tipsy ipsy and dipsy
I drink through the crippling bits

Can't stand up so red for bed
Before I know it I'm off my head
Gin and Tonic that's ironic
Tenants Super in a stupor not so duper

Lovely fella loves his Stella
'Avin' a ball it began to stall
Coming home late at night
Ten Black Russians a ton of Snakebite
Taboo and Mirage 'avin' it large
Then struck by White Lightenin'
Feelin' green in a Midori desert
This is frightening should go home
My head started to groan

Vodka shot oh why not?
Rum n coke I shouldn't joke
He said deck him so I Triple Sec'd him
Wee dram of a man more black than tan

A double whiskey was always risky
Just drink don't think
Burping my way through work
Smelling like the jerk
Hiccupping my way through marriage
Her going berserk

Yep the drink's lost it fizz the pumps have dried up
I'll drink not think just another sup

Feelin' down in one and only lonely at the bar
One for the road one for the car
I drove got driven to drink didn't stop
To think when I necked it gulped it swallowed it
And clunk-clicked it

I'm as drunk as a skunk the door's off its binges
Pissed as a newt all she does is whinges
Last orders she announced wiping the head off
My quivering lips that promised myself
Just another couple of sips

My hangover cure doesn't work any more
The headache I've got must have been that last shot
Dehydrated by life nearly fainted the wife
Won't clean up my mess anymore

Off my face and couldn't face it
Spinners aren't winners and finally realising
We drink to celebrate for fun and socialising and
Sometimes we drink to forget

The rest is history the future a mystery until

I don't drink to forget

THE GREAT BRITISH BONUS

Back in the day when they invented this system
A man in his wisdom pulled the chain on the cistern
Eureka he cried I've discovered a theory
Of taking people's money without question or query
So he put it in a safe and gave a little interest
Gave it back when you wanted behaved with disinterest
That's how it used to work but now things have changed
I'm even having trouble getting a mortgage arranged

Before they were friendly my mates and dead sociable
Now they appear cold and nothing's negotiable
Economics tells me that the dice you all shake
Are weighted without numbers yer' all on the take
How could it be that you were all so trusted?
And how does it feel now you've been busted?
Sure you don't give a hoot how the rest of us feel
The fact we all ended up with this shittiest of deals
But in your game rewards seem to be given for failure
Like changing gears on a bike but without a derailleur

Bankers wankers make me wanna puke
Put 'em all together press the button marked nuke

Yes we'd be screwed without you boys in the city
Just wish you'd share it out some more put it back into the kitty
You don't need the Ferrari or the mansion in Surrey
You don't need the Gucci or the Rolex don't worry
Invest with your money by all means who cares?
I'm not really concerned how you manage your affairs
But when you have our savings it changes the game
As well as our Cabinet you're also to blame
So come on you bankers take down the disguise
Say sorry we're tired of these secrets and lies

My mate in the know says the *bonus* is back
So get ready you poor people
You're under attack
The bonus is back and you're under attack
Get ready you bankers
You're in for some flack
Scruples and morals are something you lack

So get ready you poor folk
You're under attack

Bankers wankers make you wanna puke
Put 'em all together press the button marked nuke

GREAT BRITISH SPORT

Who would have guessed this time last year
That British sport would be looking so rosy?
In the medal cupboard of body parts
My sporting heart feels proper cosy

You know what I mean it makes you proud
In a soldiery kind of way
We go into battle predicting we'll lose
It must be our sense of fair play

But this year is very different
And now we have the belief
Passion commitment and confidence
Not the usual shaking leaf

Where do I start what a phenomenal summer?
The best we've ever seen
I hate the thought of Chelsea blues
But we salute you John Terryeeeee

Another is Bradley Wiggins
And all his skinny crew
Le Tour de France I did a dance
How fast the Yorkshiremen flew

Next up the Olympic games
Beyond our Olympic dreams
The perfect hosts n medals to boast
We didn't fall apart at the seams

The Paralympics followed
And boy did we show true grit
I shed a tear I shouted out loud
Yes I'm proud to be a Brit!

And what did we do just after that
Upon those courts of clay?
Mr Murray we salute you for
Ruining Djokovic's day

As if that's not enough to make you weep
Your eyes start welling up
We beat the yanks for Sevvy thanks
We retained the Ryder cup

ROAST DINNER

We're all aware of yer classic roast
It's roast beef with mustard
Followed by a wedge of apple pie
And lashings of hot custard

Roast turkey succulent chicken
Roast lamb and even roast pork
They're all delicious every Sunday
Little dreams on the end of my fork

Crackling and goose fat and
Broad beans and peas
Carrots and green beans devouring with ease
Proper gravy's a must
Anything else is unjust and
Make sure there's some cauliflower cheese

Please don't mush the veg
I'm young and my teeth are real

Broccoli onions leeks and snips
Now that's yer traditional meal

Finally now I forgot to mention
The most important part of the deal
You know the thing we're famous for
Yes the ones you have to peel

A spud is good mashed is great
With butter and cream
Slap it on the plate
Though forget the rest we know what's best
It's all about the roasties
Gorgeous and crispy and fluffy inside
They are what *matters* the mosties

THE GREAT BRITISH SHED

It's 8pm and I'm back in bed
I was up at four tidying the shed
Polishing brass and shaking my head
At the drip that came down the glass

That cheeky leak left a streak so oblique
He was joined by two others they became a clique
Somehow I managed to wipe it down
Watertight now the best shed in town

It's got various uses dependent on needs
Some days a sanctuary others good deeds
The size is an issue I'd love it to be bigger
But the missus isn't sure about me bringin' in a digger

I commented and serenaded her to some degree
But she wouldn't have a word of it I couldn't make her see
That if I had the chance to build a shed something more impressive
She'd have the chance to store some crap and I'd be less depressive

Gardening equipment rawl plugs and useless bits of wood
Old bits of motors none of them any good
Engine oil sump oil chain oil and spanners
Paint stripper car sprays a couple of dodgy hammers

You wouldn't believe the amount of stuff I've hoarded over the years
If she found out I'd get a clout and be straight out on me ears
The shed is where I go when I'm ousted from the house
The family thinks they're kicking me out but really I've got nouse

The TVs the video games the constant drone
I'm off my love I've had enough going to my moan-free zone
There's the radio and magazines who knows maybe a smoke?
I'll do what I want because I can an undisturbed happy bloke

Coz me and the shed we have a deal a bond in my head
He keeps me sane in moments of pain and stores my valued lead
The older I get the closer we become
The hours spent together in that long summer sun

At one in my shed my own clutter my crap
No interfering or I'll give you a slap
Sacrosanct is this church of the great divine
It's holier than thou with some home made wine

Alone in my tardis talking to the plants
Cobwebs and spiders and sometimes red ants
You know where you stand between you and your shed
He doesn't give you grief and get into your head

Eight by four is all one ever needs
Make sure it's sturdy and free of weeds
There'll never be another like yer classic shed
Given the chance inside I'd construct a small bed

Just me myself and the shed

What could be better than a small comfy bed?

THE M1

You're the spine that keeps us moving
You're the backbone of our nation
You're a blessing to all light hauliers
You give the gift of transportation
Like an old disused airfield
I loved you in 1980
But now you've changed from cream to black
You ain't nowhere near as dainty
Those rumbles you made
Left others in the shade forget the dual carriageway
You were the first you'll be the last
The all original motorway
You're toes begin at Brent Cross
At Watford where's the gap?
That bottleneck up near Derby
No need to check the map
Dodgy bogs up near Leeds
Luton wastes my time
I'm blue when the journey comes to an end

At Newcastle-UPON-Tyne

No there's nothing you can't tell me
About our glorious M1
One thing's for sure I know for a fact
I'm gonna miss him when I'm gone

Don't diss him when I'm gone

The exceptional M1

THE GREAT BRITISH SILENCE

Seen but not heard
I'm a child how absurd
We like to keep shtum
It's not that we're glum
Just quiet and mainly reserved

Sweep it under the rug
Your heartstrings will tug
Keep up that guard
Your heart is rock hard
You're the Great British silence

Shh is a word we often use
Quiet and sensible forming orderly queues
Keep it buttoned fingers on lips
Shut yer trap and eat yer chips

The service is dreadful
And the food tastes awful

No capacity for complaint
Embarrassed restraint
We do the Great British silence

This generation can change it
Open its hearts and rearrange it
Better out than in
Take it all on the chin
Got nothing to lose I'd wage it

Emotionally depressed
Everything's suppressed
Don't let it all out
Don't scream and shout
You're the Great British silence

THE GREAT BRITISH HANGOVER

Can't face me job rancid taste in me gob
'Ad too much booze so I'm hittin' the snooze
She's on six two so 'asn't a clue
I'm behaving just the way I choose

I said never again course I was lyin'
Pissed as a newt without so much as tryin'
I was totally smashed we got totally mashed
Obviously now I feel like I'm dyin'

I make the same mistake over and over
I forget that feeling of yer classic hangover

You'd think by this stage I'd be starting to learn
Whose shout is it now?
Must be someone's turn
I'm sweaty I know and my words are too slow
And my viz has a permanent gurn

Crouching in cupboards sliding down walls
Fumbling through files avoiding key calls
Hiding in storerooms treating 'em like tombs
And look at the state of my eyeballs

I make the same mistake over and over
I'm the perfect example of yer classic hangover

Asleep on the bus with my unshaven cheeks
I 'aven't felt this bad for nearly two weeks
Lookin' like death mouth with dodgy breath
Appearing just like one of the freaks
If you pardon my burping my farting too
The toilet's engaged by you know who
I use all the roll I'm permanently on the bowl
And it's me who's blocked the staff loo

Yes I make the same mistake over and over
You can see me comin' Mr Hangover
I make the same mistake over and over
I just can't shake him off the British hangover

FOR THE LOVE OF GOLF

It was introduced to me by a friend of mine this silly game of golf
He told me it was an obsessive hobby by the way his name was Rolf
I never knew about this game so never played it as a kid
Never knew the meaning of the Ryder Cup but I bet Lee Westwood did

I hack away to my heart's content you know this dye is cast
I'm as useless as a chocolate fireguard from the first tee to the last
I think I've got 'what it takes' but I can *never* deliver the goods
Unlike the best we've ever seen that lad is Tiger Woods

Doesn't matter how much I practice my stroke's a waste of space
Yes I've had a million lessons and I still can't judge the pace
I'll play in any weather I'm a die hard to the cause
Like Christmas is to winter I'm your golfing Santa Clause

I'll play with mates friends and strangers just to feel that glory
I'm happy playing by myself but that's another story
You'll wait for me on every fairway you'll wonder what's goin' on
You'll ring the bell oh what the hell this game is draggin' on

I often struggle in bunkers I'm lame when I'm on the tee
Wouldn't it be great to hit the ball like Luke or Montgomery
Ten six down we're not gonna panic you're solid Justin Rose
Sorry yanks you lost the cup that's yer golf that's the way it goes

Week after week month after month like a dog without a bone
Year after year decade after decade and still no improvement shown
The missus says it's pathetic but I know she's being coy
I reckon she's got a thing or two for that young lad McIlroy

European players like Hanson and Colsaerts never seem to falter
I've so much respect for Molinari there's no doubting Ian Poulter
McDowell Kaymer Garcia and the captain Jose Maria
The courage they showed the other night it made me shed a tear

Who gives a hoot we won the comp and now I'm having a bevvy
I nearly forgot you can't mention golf without a mention for Sevvy
He must have pulled some favours up there when we won the Ryder Cup
Drink and be merry celebrate with some sherry coz our numbers just came up

Once in a while I might be on fire and roll it straight in the cup
But mainly I'm a boss-eyed loser I should really just give up
So the next time I feel like crying I'll remember those words from Rolf
He said it's an obsessive game my mate this silly game of golf

This crazy game of golf

This glorious game of golf

TRAFFIC WARDEN

Along with special policemen you're the dirt in this town
You wear a bright uniform so unlike your brain you clown

All you do is walk around
Disqualified to walk round town
The training you 'ad must've been 'ard
What did you do? Walk 'round the yard?
Don't you worry traffic warden I'll just get a taxi
And see this ticket you daft pricket you can stick it up yer jaxi

Warden warden what does it mean?
It means oddity with lobotomy and a devil machine
Print out print out fast as you like
Next time I'll ride 100 miles on my bike
Oh don't you worry Mr Warden I'll just hail a taxi
Take this ticket take my money and shove 'em up yer jaxi

Excuse for a job it's not your fault?
You're a pain and I hate you
You sting me like salt
Go waddle you fatty why aren't you thin?
You're chunky for some reason where 'av you bin?

Hiding in butchers and crouchin' in bins?
Talkin' on the radio in cahoots with your twins?
You're a warden for god's sake all you do is fine
That and your amazing talent for staring at yellow lines

Oh don't fear Mrs Warden I'll just grab a taxi
And that clamp you just ordered you can stick that up yer jaxi

The tow truck that came actually put you to shame
At least the drivers were normal apologetic not lame
They looked very professional knew what they were doing
Unlike yourself you need a damn good shoeing

How can you look in the mirror sleep so soundly at night?
Surely you've a head full of people givin' you loads of shite
Please don't feel offended at my obvious misbehaviour
A bit like Jesus Christ you're doomed without a saviour

Next time you decide to give *me* a ticket
Just think about this rhyme
My missus knows your boss you'll be fired
The meter's up this time

So Mr Traffic Warden I'm just gonna take this taxi
And along with the wiper over that ticket
You can stick 'em both up yer jaxi

INSURANCE

I went to the garage the other day
To put a new tyre on the car
When he said d'you want insurance with that?
I replied this has gone too far
I think it's a great idea was the next thing that he said
So I casually took my pistol out and shot him in the head

Coz I've had enough of yer ruddy insurance
Yes I've had it up to here
I've had enough of your annual premiums pal
I'm not paying for another year

Insure the dog the fridge and the bog
What planet are you on?
You'll insure my mouth against it swearing?
Sounds like an 'effing con
Before insurance what did we do?
How did we actually survive?

I'll tell you how we had respect
You'd leave yer bike out on the drive

Coz I've had enough of yer bloomin' insurance
It's stupidly overpriced
Knockin' on the doors of innocent folk
Your manner's overly nice

Insure the puppy your teeth and the loan
They won't pay you out you'll be out on your own
They'll squeal and they'll squirm and make it a pain
In the end you'll be sorry you ever made the claim
They're gangsters they're monsters just taking our cash
That contract you signed it went straight in the trash

Coz we've had enough of yer dodgy insurance
You know where you can stick it
This habit we've gotten into
You know we've got to kick it

It's the only thing you pay for
And never actually own
It's a total outright rip off evidence has shown
Goin' abroad we get insured get back to the insured home
Insure your kettle insure your headache
Insure your garden gnome

Having proper insurance
I know it makes so much sense
All I'm saying is let's stop paying
No I'm not insuring the fence!!!

Well finally I've found my insurance company
An honest one at last
Said there's nothing they can't insure
And they can even insure the past

Now wouldn't that be a blast?

BRITS ABROAD

We've always loved our travelling
Even before Ryanair
So get ready destinations
This summer we'll all be there

We love to holiday and camp and board
We're always ready to roam
But we take it one step further us
And invest in a holiday home

Colonising your countries
We're totally there to stay
We probably invented timeshare
In our very British way

Only mad dogs and Englishmen
We go out in that midday sun
Forget the cream forget the shade
Getting burnt to a crisp is fun

How can you not see the fun in that?
Slapping each other on the back
Lookin' like a lobster with no after-sun
And my face is about to crack

Abroad with the broad
Or a jolly with the nippers
We're natural born travellers and
Experienced day-trippers

You can't keep us in
We're desperate to get out
We enjoy leaving the country
That's what we're all about

Because we've always loved our travelling
Even before that Ryanair
So get ready you destinations
This summer we'll all be there
Try and stop us if you dare
We'll definitely be going somewhere

BRIT KIDS DOWN THE PITS

Lying in your smuggley bed
With your Snap Crackle and Pop
Imagine waiting months and months
Just to suck on a lollypop?
I would throw you down the pits
Without a doubt you'd get the squits
You'd forget you're so large
You'd learn we're in charge
I'd dump you straight down the pits

Bringin' in a wage at a tender age
I'm trying to gauge if you get this page
I'm talking to you maybe seven or eight
The words are simple that way you'll relate
Okay that word was a little long
But I'm bigger than yer dad
And twice as strong
And if you ask him about the kids

Who went down the pits
He'll tell you they were braver
Than a hundred Brad Pitts

You've no idea how bad it was
How nothing was ever fair
Just be thankful you're feeling warm enough
And breathing in fresh air
You've having it good
Coz they fought for your blood
You unappreciative little mucker you dare
Snap crackle pop go your dreams in the night

And you'll never know what is unfair

And you'll never know how a kid feels

When the kids got the crappiest of deals

QUEEN IS ACE

The Queen is ace so serene in her royal place
A miss-spelt palace with a poison challis for a job
She's a grafter though Queenie
No sickies nay days off definitely not a meanie ask the staff
They get paid *and* have a right royal laugh

La Regina travels - a lot
She's in it for the long haul
Imagine a rock n roll tour lasting a lifetime?
Rollin Stones? Eat yer hearts out
She's rock n roll is Queeno
Rock
And Roll

She knows *how* to roll
Mixing it with all and sundry
Globetrotting from Monday to Sunday she stays the course
Does more than her bit
She's no idea what it means to quit

She's cool is our Queen

The ice maiden solid state head never bowed shoulders straight
No quiver no shaking no Zimmer no faking she covers the ground
With consummate ease and everybody's quaking in their new shiny
Shoes as she walks the line and disapproves if she chooses but she
Never does

The queen is a pro

We've never seen her go never seen her weep never seen her undies
And never seen her sleep
That bloke in her room I mean wham crash boom
Ever been alone in the bedroom?

She's got balls The Queen

She never falls from grace and probably says it even when it's soup
I'm saying she's humble
She doesn't mumble or stumble on her words
In other words she's the perfect voice

I reckon she's better than the Pope
Up there with JFK Mandela John Lennon and maybe even Ghandi
Just better than anyone else you can think of
Who's alive still working
I'm surprised that we don't have Queen TV
I'd watch it

Bet she's brilliant at trivial pursuits bet she plays monopoly and bet she doesn't gamble except for a fiver at Royal Ascot and The Grand National

Don't think I don't know you your Royal Highness
You wipe you royal bum clean your royal teeth and dribble royal dribble in your blissful royal sleep just like the rest of us

My granny knows you better than you know yourself Queenie
And she gives me the info
The lowdown
The scrapbooks they're my secret
My granny and her scrapbooks

She's the same age as you Mrs Queen

She tells me you're a grafter Queenie and I believe her

A proper grafter

Old School

FOOTY

Of course we were the founders
Of this the most beautiful game
The English I mean the Scottish okay British
One could argue we're one and the same

There's nothing we don't know about football
We've got everything in our locker
We sold the game around the world
We exported the pastime of soccer

Our fans are loyal to the core
Our chanting is the best
The television coverage
Is far better than the rest

We haven't deployed any fences
Unlike our European neighbours
So if we're made out to be hooligans
It's not for our pitch-side capers

Ever wondered why the foreigners
Love our game so much?
Because the fans get so close to the players
So close you can even touch

The premier league the best in the world
Ever wondered how that could be?
It's because of the pace the mixes of race
Oh and the enormous salary

Yes the Spanish are hot on our heels
With Messi the world's loved up
But one of these days we'll change our ways
Who knows we'll win the World Cup

I'm being stupid now I'll shut up

UK CARNIVAL QUEEN

Not even 14 she was a carnival queen
Her parents were missing always had been
Mixed up and twisted with an itch she couldn't scratch
Anyone could go in there she left the door off the latch

Of course people filled their boots not surprising she's up the duff
Imagine the site of a 12lb baby squeezin' outta that tiny muff

Not a pleasant thought I know but who could be the dad?
One of many said the nurse who'd just replaced her pad
So twelve different fathers arrived to see the birth
All of them excited to see whose spunk had worked

Crammed together into this tiny room
The doctor the midwife the potential grooms
The brother the sister her best mate Mandy
The gas and air it came in handy

She huffed and puffed and kicked and screamed
The lump wouldn't move and so it was deemed
Epidural's the one and then some pethadene
All in the room were thinking what might have been

With one last push the child shot out
Past all the fathers who were in no doubt
That this was a baby no one had ever seen
Twelve different colours even a green gene

So the question arose well who is the dad?
None of them admitted it was all rather sad
Coz apparently a gang bang had become commonplace
Twelve different blokes all painting her face

Twelve different guns all shooting their load
You could hear the orgasms over the road
So the council has visited been understanding
Given them a 12 bedroomed house nice big landing

Now the carnival queen lives the carnival dream
Twelve separate incomes she's not daft it would seem
She knew all along about the multi-father scheme
It's for people who drink lots of different cream

Now the daughter's just turned ten learnt off her mother
Up the duff once again
No abortion for them
Just the dream

The life of the carnival queen

Not caring where she's been

TRADITIONAL

Never grasped the concept of Morris dancing
Often gawped at the sight of these men
I don't take part in that prancing
I prefer a more modern-day zen

We should take a leaf outta the Germans book
Those guys are on a mission
They move forward adapt and change
They're not shackled by their own tradition

I'll happily play bloomin' pooh sticks
If it keeps the little ones happy
I'll fall in line and take out the bins
But please love you change the nappy

I'll wash the car and I'll walk the dog
I'll go out and earn a crust
I'll fix the sink and mow the lawn
Put yer feet up I've got it sussed

When it comes to tradition
I'm the traditional sort but with
A funny kind of twist
Things like washing pots and pans
They won't be sorely missed

I've said my piece and now it's time
To end this polite rendition
The silliest sayings and the daftest acts
Don't do 'em just because it's tradition

CAMORON

This is my political rant I've only got the one
After all why waste time thinking about CaMoron?

First of all it's not your fault you're just the one in power
You're a metaphor for all before yes you're just as effin' dour
How can we respect you and all your shower?
The only politics I respect was Churchill's finest hour

Yep this is my political rant and I've only got the one
But I'm not squandering all my time deliberating Camoron

Second up you've mucked it up like a smashed egg on the slab
You screwed up the London traffic ever tried grabbin' a cab?
The village shop and post office you've made them very sparse
Those policies you promised us have disappeared right up your arse

So this is my political rant I've only written one
I'm not gonna waste any more of my ink on that stinky Camoron

Thirdly worldly wise I reckon clueless and spineless the lot
If I begin to dwell on them too much my angry brain begins to clot
Call it off I'm done already this impractical political stuff
I've had my fill of British politics you know I've had enough

So this has been my political rant you know there's only one
You know it's easy to waste your time mulling over Camoron

Finally now you're getting the picture clearly it's looking dismal
You're paying for their idle spoils they've made your life abysmal
They paid the banks they never said thanks any faith in you has gone
You're just a ponse with a ponsey bonse you moron Camoron

So now you've heard my political rant and I'm not the only one
Who thinks this way about losing their time
On that loser Camoron

That schmoozer CaMoron

SALUTE TO CLARKEY

John Cooper Clarkey
A barrel of laughs in Manchester gaffs
Only he's the real deal my mate Tarkey
Not met 'im yet don't wanna be a threat
More voices the merrier I'm not a terrier
But northern yes northern you bet

I'm comfortable down south
Even with this mouth
Don't want to appear somewhat darky
Not in the shadow of the Clarkey
I feel like a cock
Like a dick in the dock
Will the judge Clarkey take stock?
I'm not sure if I care
But I care that's he's here

The visionary that is our Clarkey

Clarkey was a family throughout my junior years
Three big brothers one of them with ears
We used to call him Tarkey not sure why
Maybe like an otter he was a little bit shy

Shy is the guy who makes the chicken pie
Scared of opening wide his mouth
And shouting at the sky
I thought I'd introduce myself
I'm feelin' rather shy
It's me that is Clarkey
To meet you yes I'd die
And if there's one thing I'll sing
Thank god you don't wear khaki
You are the word I only just heard
You're John Cooper Clarkey

I'm Dom Super Sarky

STUDENTS

No one feels sorry for students
And I can't say I blame 'em
Blame's not a word I like to lay
I prefer to try and shame 'em

Lazy crazy all they do is drink
Like sausage and dogs there's a tenuous link
Between student and studying and trying real hard
A place where most of 'em find themselves barred

Soap dodgers smelly gits never like to wash
Always late with assignments
As if they're under the cosh
How can we relate?
When all we do is giving
You're young I suppose
And one day who knows
You might even work for a living

Student moan student groan
Don't take that student tone
I'm not feeling sorry for you *or* your mates
Not least your student loan

Though sounds like they might have something right
Don't have to graft they get drunk every night
I could live that life given half a chance
Off yer 'ead meeting birds to the buffalo stance

When we were at school we all poked fun
At the idea of learning it just wasn't done
We scoffed at brains and yes we all laughed
At the boy in the corner with the book not daft

Let's encourage the student to educate and learn
And let's not discourage them at every turn
We've got it so wrong the system's defunct
Like Ashton Kutcher you know they've been punked

STAG SLAGS

Stag shag stag slag stick it up his arse
He's on a British stag do and likes to 'av it large
We're making sure 'e bangs a dwarf so we can watch with pleasure
And take some video on our phones just for our good measure

The beer and spirits flow like there's no tomorrow
And the groom senses doom and guilt and sorrow
The boys are pissed already and they've drawn up the list
Of stuff they'll do birds they'll bang and dealers they'll enlist

The staggy's in town roll up roll up
We're wandering aimlessly down and up
There's booze going round and drugs a plenty
Labidos full and consciences empty

Where's all the action? We need some fanny
One of the lads nearly chats up a tranny
Off the leash for the first time in a while
Bound to stray away all she has to do is smile

The lights go down and the group begins to splinter
They go their separate ways and who knows what they're inter?
Pockets full of dollars and sacks full of spuds
Off for a lap dance and expecting the goods

Downin' the booze at twenty quid a pop
Costs you thirty just to look and then the stuff on top
And the rest of the boys spend the rest of the pot
This is turning real ugly double tequila shot

Peer pressure lad culture towing the line
You've gotta drink a yard of beer and then a box of wine
Rules and regs don't you like the snake that's in her bum?
Don't be such a pussy lad and join on in the fun!

We know we're getting seedy but that's the main reason
At home we're just sterile we're never in season
We won't even remember what 'appens this torrid night
So even if you saw us be sure to keep it tight

Coz what 'appens on the staggy stays just where it should
We wouldn't want a staggy blurt coz then there'd be staggy blood

The stag is just the reason so that we can all *play* away
Of course we love a wedding darling it's a *very* special day

FALLING APART

My sense of smell is disappearing my hair has started to thin
The dentist says my gums are receding I'm lookin' toothless when I grin
The bags are getting heavier my eyes are goin' dicky
Even reading the morning paper has become a little tricky
The hairs have started sprouting on my nose and in my ears
Making me look like someone else who's way beyond his years

Yes I'm falling apart right at the seams
Would love to be younger in my jealous dreams
I've been to the doctor yes I'm falling apart
He's feeling the same we're not sure where to start

My stomach's feeling bloated my knees are turning knobbly
My feet are proving useless my walk is getting wobbly
My back is getting stiffer unlike the other thing down there
My cheeks are not as rosy I'm spending more time in my chair
I'm not as regular as before my bones are sounding creaky
I'm sleeping less and waking up with a bladder that's a little leaky

Yes I'm falling apart right at the seams
Would love to be fitter in my jealous dreams
I've been to the doctor yes I'm falling apart
He's feeling the same no clue where to start

Can't cycle uphill I'm staying on the flat
Used to run for miles now I jog like a twat
I've taken to having a massage and a bit of osteopathy
Visiting various clinics meditation and homeopathy
My nails are getting harder my skin is going pale
The wrinkles are increasing this boat is setting sail
My hands are looking spindly my nipples are all droopy
The brain cells are decreasing and for sure I'm going loopy
In fact I know I've lost the plot coz just the other day
I forgot my keys my phone my dog and even what to say

Yes I'm falling apart right at the seams
Well that's how it seems in my jealous dreams
I've had it with the doctor I've had it with this curse
Nothing I can do to put the process in reverse

Say my prayers every night live my lifestyle just right
Forget my pain enjoy my pleasure
And just for my good measure
Get a surgeon to quote me outright

Make me younger and bolder overnight

THE BRITISH FAITH

I have faith
Believe me I have faith
I'm faithful to myself and I'm faithful to others
I'm faithful to my partner to my kids to my parents

I have faith
I have faith in something that's hard to describe
Yes I look up to the heavens when I question my faith
Because that's from where it came
I do believe our answers are out there
As stardust

I have faith in humanity
Most of the time
I know it only takes the actions of one human being to cause misery for many
And if that human being is determined enough then
They will have their way

But I still have faith

I believe
I believe - but I don't need religion
Religion is here and now it's not in the skies or in books
It's being
My religion is being

Here's an idea
What about a new religion?
We'll call it THE FAITH
Starting with THE BRITISH FAITH
We have no building or shrine
Our church is our community our homes towns and cities
We are all brothers and sisters

Go on I dare you
Leave your fellow Muslims
Leave your fellow Christians
Leave your fellow Catholics
Your Protestants Buddhists and Islamists

Leave your places of safety repression and rules

I dare you just leave

Walk towards the light

Come join THE BRITISH FAITH

Even if you're not British

Because life starts here

Real living starts here

It's time for a new religion

TOWN IS TOP

Manchester…manchesta…manchesdo
Manchesdo without raaaaain is like
Shikaaaaago without wiiiind
Manchesdo as got great muuuusic
Clubbin man 90's man rockin
Top tunes
Manchesdo's got great gigs always as 'ad
Undergrowwwwwwnd yeah?
In Manchesdo we're dead naaaasally
We don't talk down here
We talk
Up 'ere coz we're dead naaaaaasally
It's all up top yeah?
Top
Manchesdo as top baaaaaars
Manchesdo is top banaaaaaanA
Friendly faces
In Manchesdo we're avvin it
We've always ad it

Laaaaaaaaaarge
No one 'as it like us right?
Dead riiiiight riiiiight?

In Manchesdo we got footbaaaall
It's the lifeblood yeah?
The blood - of life

In Manchesdo we got a sense o uuuuuuuuma
You can av the crack yeah?
Coz it's always raiiiiinin right?
No point bein' miserable

In Manchesdo it's got it all
Yeah we got gangs we got uddies ooo asn't? But we got
The velodrome yeah? We got media ciaaaay
We got the gay village and we got one and two in the premiership
How top is that?

In Manchesdo we got The Street we got the Trafford ceno
And we got the curry miiiiiiile

If you want a curry n a top laugh come to Manchesdo

Manchesdo is now less than two ours from London
It's alright London fer a laugh n that but it's not town

Town's town man – 'as bin for time

Come n av it

It's top

TEA N BICKIES

I love a mug of tea me
In a morning first thing after the wee
Wet yer whistle suck on a Rich Tea
I can drink a gallon of tea easily
Don't want that flowery crap
At least three minutes with the bag
Bourbon cream custard cream
Don't need sugar just a spot of milk
Take a flask to work
Dunk some bickies big slurp
Gran likes a cuppa too
Pot of best china'll do
Shortbread on the side
Chocolate hob nobs in the wings
McVities as standard
One of those bickie things
Gimme classic builders'
Plenty of colour
Don't use the skimmed stuff

Tastes less fuller

Elevenses me and brew
Takes me through
To lunch crumble crunch
To another tea or two
And on with the afternoon
Maybe a digestive or macaroon
Kettle's boiling dinnertime
Time for the box of Teatime
Snaffle a Jaffa cake
How many teas can you take?
Couple of cookies one for the road
One before bed to settle the head
Dreamin of dunkin' while I'm snoring
Lookin forward to tea and bickies
In the mornin'

Where would I be without my tea?
I'm stopping
This is getting boring

NO TV

Imagine a world without a screen
How would the UK feel?
Bet we'd scream and shout
Bet we'd slit our wrists
Right now you can picture the deal

Lifeless and helpless and dying
We wouldn't know how to be
Imagine our planet and
Where we'd be at?
In a world without TV

This world without TV

THE WAR

I don't want to bore you about the war
But my grandad was there and he knew for sure
That life at this time was cheap and dispensable
Perhaps the motives were somewhat incomprehensible

But from what he tells me on the odd occasion
You needed to have a certain persuasion
Going to war wasn't taken lightly
It's the bravest of acts with images so unsightly

Seeing your mate being shot or just simply blown to bits
Scrawny limbs hanging off those battling Brits
Decapitated bodies for all to see
Who'll tell his wife and the rest of the family?

Keep calm and carry on you know we'll all get through it
You've seen the state of the fat now learn how to chew it
The boy who left came a back a man
Although at the time he never knew it

And this is how it was in the war
I don’t want to be a bore my final words about the war
My grandad could talk forever more
The lives we lost the sacrifices made
So now our lives are cosy

Should be made law to remember the war

Don’t forget why your life is so rosy

BORDER COUNTRY

England Ireland Scotland Wales
We've got no borders but everyone fails
To realise we're different nations apart
Yes we're neighbours with borders
We have been from the start
But people abroad just see us as one
So what? It's four countries?
Great Britton?

Yes take a look at our national flag
All three or four together
Without borders but with borders
Sort of birds of a feather
England is pleasant and gentle and
In Wales the girls are frisky
Northern Ireland is small and cute and
Scotland has all the whiskey

The English the Irish the Scottish the Welsh
We're four different people in one
So the next time you visit when you've come from afar
Remember to get out of London

Coz GB is different and culturally diverse
Go across those invisible borders
I'm telling you now go see all four corners
It's almost like going abroaders

The stamp in the passport says the UK
Yet another confusing term
Don't worry it means United Kingdom
It's something you'll eventually learn

Because we have borders without borders
Four countries in one
We all live together so it's a sort of a con
It must be more profitable to be this kind of entity
Or maybe we're just stubborn
We want to keep our own identity

Yes we've got borders without borders
We're nationalists I'd say
Ultimately it's not our choice
The politicians will have their way

The United Kingdom of Great Britain and Northern Ireland
Is how it should be said
What a mouthful how confusing is that?
Now I'm putting the subject to bed

OLD PEOPLE

Rapidly changing demographics
People are living longer
Developing countries need help
One billion over sixties
Older folk are the fastest growing sector
One child policy people
Sleep walking into a problem
You'll be old before you're rich
Save for the future
Raise the retirement age
Public policy needs to change
Population ageing
Fewer children living longer
More dependents than people working
Who's going to care?

Who's going to do the care?

Does anyone care?

They feel like a burden on the state and at home
It's not their fault they're living so long
They'll die in the streets
Won't get their bottoms wiped
More care homes than family homes
Robots caring for old people
Not facing responsibility to look after our elders
I wanna be cared for when I get old
Don't wanna be left in a box-room that's cold
Old people they're everywhere

Watch out

THE GREAT BRITISH SEASIDE

You're from another era you used to be the top
Today you're just a faded memory
Jaded and shut up shop

You've spent the last 50 years
Struggling for survival
The British seaside's dead on its knees
I wish we could have a revival

St Davids Beaumaris
Bournemouth and Rhyl
Formerly great seaside towns
But nowadays it's not the drill

Newquay Torquay Aberystwyth and Dunoon
Paignton and Brixham the occasional honeymoon
Rothesay Lamlas and Whiting Bay
Millport and Campbeltown
They've all had their day

Cleethorpes Mablethorpe
This rhyme has got a rhythm
Margate and Skeggy and don't forget Lytham

Without Scarborough and Whitby
Where would we be?
Probably in Tenby or Clacton-on-Sea
Isle of White Isle of Mull
Once lovely places
But now they're dull

Torbay
Bexhill-on-Sea
Ever been to Broadstairs?
I went once I was such a dunce
Now I'm having Weston-Super-Nightmares

Which coast this week?
I'm always torn
Weymouth Minehead
Quite possibly Eastbourne

Bridlington Morecambe Llandudno or Cromer
Look in these places you'll find the odd loner

Southend-on-Sea the golden smile
Blackpool Tower's a little bit wonky
Picture postcard stuff so kiss me quick
Don't forget that ride on the donkey

Sorry if I forgot to mention you
No doubt your seaside town
Is suffering the way the others do
These words will make you frown

Is it the end of the seaside town?
It's fighting for its survival
Blow the budget airlines out of the skies
And we'd be lookin' at a seaside revival

A British coastal revival

INFO

Thank you for reading my book

If you'd like to contact the author or to

View more poetry or to

Order copies of this book please visit the website

templefields.com

or

britishpoems.co.uk